The Supervisor's Guide to Human Relations and Communication

The Supervisor's Guide to Human Relations and Communication

Michael D Santonino III
&
Frank J Villa Jr

ISBN: 1548691445
ISBN 13: 9781548691448

TO KIM PEI, MY WIFE
TO MY UNCLE FRANK, MY FAMILY, AND MY ITALIAN
HERITAGE

TABLE OF CONTENTS

Introduction

Today, many small businesses do not have the resources provided by training and development departments for formal supervisory and management programs. This little book was designed for the hourly worker who is promoted to a supervisory position without any formal education, experience, or mentorship program. Similarly, educated workers who catapult into managerial roles and responsibilities without the practice of being managers may find this an informative guidebook for supervisors. This book offers suggestions designed to improve skills as a supervisor in human relations and communication with fellow supervisors, subordinates, and associates. An easily navigable reading format allows the reader to start at the beginning, or flip to any chapter to fit their immediate needs. All chapters have practical tips, guidelines, and suggestions for supervisors to become better at their jobs; or at least, to more easily understand people and the roles and responsibilities of a supervisor.

Acknowledgements

To all the persons who have helped in the preparation and publication of this book "grazie mille" (many thanks).

This little book would not be possible without the loving support of my wife, Kim Pei, who has endured my fitful temperament with the patience of a saint. 我深爱着你

The Supervisor's Guide to

HUMAN RELATIONS
AND COMMUNICATION

Chapter 1

THE SUPERVISOR

*"The principle object of management
should be to secure the maximum
prosperity for the employer,
coupled with the maximum
prosperity for each employee"*

-FREDERICK WINSLOW TAYLOR (1911)*

A supervisor is any person who directs the work of one or more people. The supervisor must align his or her beliefs, values, norms, and practices with the viewpoint of management, as a supervisor is part of management. In the past, a supervisor was respected and obeyed because of their authority over subordinates. The supervisor made decisions and the subordinates' only responsibilities were to obey – not question, not argue – simply obey. Today, this has changed: as workers seek independence, they need to identify with their organizations. Employees seek more active roles in decision-making that affects them person-ally, and the supervisor who desires to understand their employees' needs and is responsive to these needs will be respected – not only because the supervisor is the boss, but also because of the supervisor's knowledge, abilities, com-passion, and understanding. A fundamental change in the workforce attitude over the last two decades or more is that leadership today must be earned, not merely demanded.

The path before becoming a supervisor normally involves a promotion process or an assigned job skill (e.g., technical). The moment one becomes a supervisor, there is a need to rely on other people to accomplish productive work. As a supervisor, the words used, inflections, and atti-tude mirrors those of the organization. That is, an individual employee's ability to make a difference within the organiza-tional unit is determined by the supervisor. The supervisor's job is measured in terms of their ability to handle people. The supervisor must balance the goal of the organization to make a profit through skillfully dealing with people in a way that will cause them to be productive willingly.

Business firms are established for the purpose of making a profit and, in dealing with people, a supervi-sor must garner high-quality and high-quantity produc-tion or service at the lowest cost possible. Therefore, the supervisor's efficiency is measured in terms of their ability to inspire cooperative effort in obtaining these goals. It was formerly common practice to acquire experience through years of contact with the job. When someone was made a supervisor, they were expected to learn through experience on the job. Little attempt was made to train supervisors in the art of handling people or incidents that occur on the job. It was generally believed that people had an intrinsic leadership quality within them and there was otherwise no way to acquire it. There is some validity to this position; but there is also validity in the idea that proper supervision may be learned, just as a technical subject may be studied and mastered. It is not necessary to spend long years of trial and effort before arriving at a reasonable degree of efficiency. Hence, any supervisor can improve in the art of handling people.

The responsibility of the supervisor is to know the people, as individuals, that they supervise -- no two people are alike. As a supervisor, your success or failure in the role requires relationship-building. This takes time, commitment, and a genuine interest on the part of the supervisor to get to know the people working for them.

Supervisors with a high level of technical competency and poor human relations skills will likely survive in a highly technical industry in design and development. Sadly, poor human relations skills can cause dissension and moral issues for workers. This differs from the counterpart – a supervisor with poor technical competency in the same industry and excellent human relations skills – who would either be removed for incompetency or transferred to a different department that recognizes the human relations skill set. In either case, the supervisor must develop a balance of technical and human relations skills to be thought of by others as a successful supervisor. A supervisor with good human relations skills that is able to communicate with people can develop genuine and trusting relationships that will sustain a department with motivated workers willing to go above and beyond for their respected supervisor. A metaphor used in management about managers' genuine engagement with employees is: *a manager that is able to crawl around the production shop floor and getting dirt under your fingernails.* This metaphor emphasizes the manager that is able to understand what is happening in manufacturing by doing. This applies to any other business not just manufacturing. There are five basic principles that cause all people to respond favorably – these are the *foundations of human relations.*

The five principles are:

1. Each employee has a right to know how they're getting along;
2. Each employee has a right to receive credit when credit is due;
3. Each employee has a right to have their talents used in the best way possible;

4. Each employee has a right to know in advance of changes that will affect them;
5. Each employee has a right to know why the job they're doing is important and how it fits into the organizational big picture.

These five *foundations of human relations* are simple devices that, when applied, bring surprising results. If a worker is doing their job incorrectly, they have the right to know how to improve. If they are doing their job properly, they have the right to be genuinely acknowledge for good work from their supervisor. A supervisor is no stronger than the people in their department. The supervisor should encourage each of their workers to reach the highest possible work efficiency. This can only be achieved by giving proper credit for ideas, suggestions, or improvements. Workers enjoy having their work reflect their importance. People like to know they are necessary to an organization in an authentic and trusting way. Most of the principles of human relations are not new; they were used during biblical times and are embodied in the Golden Rule, "Do unto others as you would have others do unto you."

There are five business aspects that executive management expects from each supervisor. They are:

1. Supervisors keep the respect and confidence of their subordinates;
2. Supervisors meet the daily quota for work completed by subordinates;
3. Supervisors maintain quality standards;
4. Supervisors keep costs down;
5. Supervisors improve the processes and methodologies used.

There are five basic human relations principles that subordinates expect from supervisors. They are:

1. Fair treatment;
2. Fair wages;
3. Good work conditions;
4. An understanding of their problems;
5. An application of the Golden Rule.

In order to meet these responsibilities, it is necessary that the supervisor:

1. Know the job;
2. Know the company policies and procedures;
3. Organize their job systematically;
4. Understand people and how to arouse their response.

In summary:

1. A supervisor is any person who directs the work of one or more people;
2. A supervisor accomplishes their tasks through people;
3. A supervisor garners the best results by dealing with people as individuals;
4. A supervisor should apply the "Foundations for Human Relations";
5. A supervisor gets the best results by following the Golden Rule;
6. A supervisor should understand the fact that each person is the most important person in the world to themselves;
7. A supervisor will get the best results usually by listening and questioning, rather than talking;
8. A supervisor's department is no stronger than the people who work in it.

Endnotes

Frederick Winslow Taylor, *The Principles of Scientific Management*, (New York: Harper & Brothers, 1911): p.7.

Earlier work from Frederick Winslow Taylor (1856-1915) during the age of scientific management addressed the notion (as poor as it was at this time) that managers thought of their employees as dispensable "cogs in the wheel" or part of the machine on the production floor. Many of the classical thoughts will never be outdated, as relevant today as back in the early 1900s to be an effective supervisor and manager.

Chapter 2

LEADERSHIP

*"Management is doing things right;
leadership is doing the right things"*

-PETER F. DRUCKER

Whenever you have people working together, there are bound to be dislikes, dissatisfactions, grievances, jealousies, misunderstandings, and even opposition to the common cause. These personnel problems give rise to the study of human relations. A supervisor grows through handling problems such as these. Success in dealing with human relations problems and causing people to respond favorably to their situation is *leadership*.

Leadership is one of the most important qualities a supervisor must possess in order to achieve efficiency. All persons may develop leadership to varying degrees. Some people seem to be born leaders; others have it thrust upon them, while most must acquire it the hard way: through conscious effort and hard work. Analysis indicates that the following traits or qualities are desirable in leadership:

1. *A logical mind* – This may be acquired through developing an orderly mind with facts and figures justifying the arrived-upon conclusions.
2. *Salesmanship* – This is of prime importance since a supervisor must constantly sell their ideas to colleagues and subordinates. In salesmanship, the supervisor learns to take the proper approach, secure favorable attention, arouse interest, create desire, answer objections, and close the sale. Real sales abilities come only with experience.
3. *Tact and diplomacy* – A leader should use tact in dealing with both superiors and subordinates since better results are obtained this way. The leader remembers always to respect the feelings of others and treats them as the leader would like to be treated if the positions were reversed.
4. *A pleasing manner and appearance* – These come largely by habit. Some people are naturally tidy and will have a neat appearance and pleasing manner, even though their apparel is of the

simplest type. Others may be dressed expensively, yet look untidy.

5. *Tolerance* – It is necessary to recognize the weaknesses of people and understand them. We must have all our employees' goodwill and, before we can expect that, it is necessary to extend ours.

6. *Good judgment* – This is based upon understanding, which comes only through practice in making decisions based on facts. Exercising good judgment is the art of being just.

7. *Impartiality* – Favoritism in dealing with people will cause resentment for both the supervisor as well as those favored. It is harmful to leadership to show bias or partiality.

8. *Cooperativeness* – In order to obtain proper results through leadership, one must be cooperative and inspire cooperation in others. .

9. *Sympathetic understanding of people* – This is developed only through accepting people as they are. Employees are human beings with strengths and faults, and react similarly to the way supervisors react in most things.

10. *Fairness and honesty* – These are best acquired through acting without emotion and with the objective of doing good for the greatest number of people.

11. *Knowledge of work* – It is important in leading others to know more about the job at hand than

any of those following. It is not necessary to know each job completely, but the supervisor should have an overall picture.

12. *Planning abilities* – This is part of a leader's work, and the ability to plan is often the difference between success and failure. Leaders should evaluate everything crucially without openly criticizing.

13. *A pleasing voice* – This may be cultivated. It aids in causing others to follow.

14. *Loyalty* – Loyalty to our workers and to our company makes for sound leadership.

It can be seen easily that, if one possesses these qualities in any appreciable degree, they have all the desired qualities for leadership.

PART ONE: DISCIPLINE

The great majority of employees want to be part of a well-organized and productive group, rather than work in a unit where leadership is remiss, rules disregarded, and standards are so low that any incentive to achieve is dampened. Employees like the challenge of productive discipline and respect the leader who provides it. Employees do not object to reasonable orders, rules, and standards. Employees have a greater sense of direction when governed by practical regulations and stimulating demands that they understand are in their own self-interest and promote the welfare of the whole organization. Employees want positive leadership that is *real*, *genuine*, and *trustworthy*. These three attributes seldom cause a serious problem of discipline because the employees or department members discipline themselves. When disciplinary problems do occur in a department or work group, they can often be traced directly to problems in leadership. A self-disciplined work group is the result of sound supervisory leadership, practiced continually, on a full-time basis. The quality of discipline in a department, work group, or among individual contributors demonstrates the proficiency of a supervisor and the standards of leadership the group is capable of obtaining. Effective supervisors seldom need to resort to formal disciplinary measures. The reason is simple: the leader shows positive leadership traits in administering instructions to the department, group, or individual through sound supervisory practices.

No employee is perfect. Equally, no manager, supervisor, or leader is perfect. No matter what the title of the position or number of years of service with the company, the fact that humans are involved in an organization make it flawed one way or another.

When discipline problems do occur, good supervisors do not allow them to linger and spread to other employees; the supervisor must take a leadership role to resolve issues in the early stages through informal means. Almost any employee, on rare occasions, may fail to observe the rules and regulation standards of the company. For example, extended break times or reporting to work late both constitute violations of rules. A supervisor would be ill-advised to take formal disciplinary steps when the infractions are minor and the employee does a good job otherwise. It is far better to observe and counsel such employees to help them improve through corrective means, rather than hastily cracking the whip.

When employees are first hired, they should be told it is mandatory for everyone to follow the rules, but should be trained and counseled until they clearly understand the rules and regulations and the purposes behind them. The new employee should also be informed of the company policy, and the supervisor should first talk with employees informally when a rule is violated. The purpose of such informal talks is to impress upon the employee that rules and standards must be observed. It is important that the employee understand this constructive aspect of company policy and the expectations of employees. Such understanding helps the employee develop a more positive attitude toward discipline. The informal talk gives the supervisor a chance to find out why the infraction occurred. There may be a valid reason why the employee came in late or overextended a coffee break. The reason could be that other employees are remaining longer at breaks and the new employee is following others' habits.

If an infraction of job standards occurs – careless work, for example – the employee may need training, be under pressure, have poor equipment, or not be adequately informed of the importance of standards. Experience has shown that often what, at first glance, looks like a willful infraction, turns out to be an explainable action by an employee who lacked information, was a victim of circumstance, needed training, had a correctable faulty attitude, or had a temporary lack of self-control. By talking with the employee, the supervisor can discover such causes of misconduct and help the employee improve. The talk can also uncover job conditions which may precipitate disciplinary problems, giving the supervisor the opportunity to correct such conditions. The utility of this informal stage is that it enables the supervisor to take corrective action without getting involved in formal faultfinding and entering negative reports into the employee's record. The employee is likely to be less resentful when corrected informally than if a formal record is made of the infraction. It is good *human relations* and *communications* to do it this way.

PART TWO: MORE THAN TALK IS REQUIRED

An informal talk with the employee is valuable only if the supervisor conducts it in a way that achieves results. If the supervisor gives the impression that the infraction is not taken seriously and that the informal talk is only a matter of routine, the employee may be inclined to repeat the offense. The supervisor must demonstrate enough sincerity and earnestness during an informal corrective interview or conversation with the employee to make it clear that a change in behavior regarding rules and standards is expected. Some supervisors mistakenly take disciplinary action when an employee's work performance is unsatisfactory – that is, action taken without knowledge of the employee's strengths and weaknesses. If an employee lacks the skills to work adequately, the remedy is further training, reassignment, demotion, or dismissal for inability to do the work.

If an employee makes real effort to improve, sufficient time should be allowed; however, if an employee lacks skill and refuses to cooperate with needed training, appropriate disciplinary action is called for. If an employee has the skill to perform but is lax, careless, and knowingly disregards work standards, stern disciplinary action or possible termination is appropriate. The most difficult dilemma a supervisor faces is when an employee is both a capable worker and a frequent violator of rules. In such a case, the supervisor will need to use all the skills necessary to align the worker with the rules before the situation gets out of control and affects other employees. The negative effect an employee can have on the morale of other employees is a key consideration, as well. The supervisor must do better to develop the employee's attitude or hire a replacement. The old saying that "nobody is irreplaceable" applies to all companies and organizations. The tradeoff costs associated with replacing an employee become irrelevant for most organizations, as it may be the only solution in the long run.

Here are some helpful tips in the hiring to firing process:

1. When hiring an employee, do not state or imply that the job is a continuous contract of employment or permanent. Even a statement like, "You are most likely to move up the rank in a few years," may be challenged in a labor court dispute.

2. If an employee has made a legitimate complaint about the department or its manager, or reported an illegal or unethical behavior in the department, do not harass the employee in any way.

3. If the organization does not have a discipline policy, write a discipline policy for your department and implement it. Take the advice of legal counsel before implementing policy.

4. If the organization does have a discipline policy, do not skip any steps required by that policy when taking formal disciplinary actions.

5. When firing an employee do not attempt to make any personal comments. For example, do not say things like, "You're a drunk and a degenerate gambler," or "You're a deadbeat dad," or "No one around here likes you." Do not say things that can enrage an employee (even if they are true).

6. Do not make any reference to a person's race, sex, nationality, appearance, color, religion, emotional state, physical state, or personal worth.
7. Do not allow the fired employee to meet with coworkers, access information systems or leave with company property.
8. Be firm, direct, and brief in the rationale for the firing.
9. Do not fire an employee without the presence of a witness.
10. Do not fire an employee unless you are meeting physically face-to-face.

Endnotes

Peter F. Drucker, *The Essential Drucker: The Best of Sixty Years of Peter Drucker's Essential Writings on Management*, (New York: Harper Business, Reissue, 2008).

The Supervisor's Guide to

HUMAN RELATIONS AND COMMUNICATION

Chapter 3

PLANNING AND CONTROL

*"It is the individual who is not
interested in his fellow men who has
the greatest difficulties in life and
provides the greatest injury to others.
It is from among such individuals
that all human failures spring."*

-ALFRED ADLER *(1932)*

Two important elements of a supervisor's work are *planning* and *control*. The efficiency of a supervisor is in direct proportion to their ability to plan and control.

In planning, the supervisor must be able to determine *what* should be done, *who* should do it, *when* it should be done, *where* it should be done, *why* it should be done, and *how* it should be done. These questions should be asked of every operation a supervisor directs.

The second fundamental element is control. Control is affected through people, either in groups or as individuals. Much of this control is done through what is known as "standard practices" or "policies" of the company. Control ensures that there is efficient and effective use of the available resources in the company so employees are successful in achieving the planned goals set by the supervisor. A supervisor should be able to analyze their job as an engineer would analyze a structure's design. The supervisor has machinery, tools, and equipment at their command, and has methods by which these tools can be used. The supervisor has time in which to use these tools, and has people to whom the various tasks can be assigned. The only variable feature involved pertains to the people. The others are constant.

There are nine rules that can be useful in establishing an organization. These rules are as follows:

1. Proper paths of authority should be established and understood by all concerned, and authority should flow through these channels in their regular order;
2. No job holder, occupying a single position, should be responsible to more than one boss directly;

3. As responsibility becomes more involved, authority should be delegated to qualified assistants;
4. Each assistant should have no more subordinates than can be effectively controlled;
5. The delegated responsibility and its resulting duties must be clearly defined and understood by all concerned to permit maximum efficiency;
6. Assistants should be given authority in keeping with the responsibility delegated to them. Every difference of opinion arising from jurisdictional disputes, regardless of how trivial, should be handled properly;
7. There should be frequent discussion between supervisors to coordinate efforts;
8. Authority between the supervisor and staff experts should be clearly defined and understood;
9. Every person should be held accountable for the responsibility delegated to them.

Once an organization is established, the supervisor's planning is not over. The supervisor must additionally prepare definite standards of performance. Every worker is entitled to know their job expectations; therefore, it is part of the supervisor's job to acquaint each worker with the required standard of performance. These standards will include tolerances allowed, percentage of defects permissible, the degree of regularity in attendance, the amount of time permitted for personal requirements, the time necessary to maintain personal equipment, etc. In other words, the organization must be composed of workers who understand the minimum requirements of their jobs and how to perform their jobs to achieve that minimum.

The supervisor can consider their job well done when they have an organization which meets the nine standards above, composed of employees who know exactly what is expected. At that time, the supervisor can spend most of their time planning and actually supervising.

FAILURE OF MANAGEMENT TO WIN EMPLOYEES' ACCEPTANCE OF RULES AND POLICIES

You can't simply post a list of "dos" and "don'ts" on a bulletin board or email announcement and consider the job done. If the public doesn't accept a law because people think it is unreasonable, the government has great difficulty enforcing it. The same is true of employees. If they think a rule is unfair or arbitrary, they resent it and may ignore it. That is why a wise supervisor makes certain every employee not only knows the rules that affect them on the job, but also understands their individual objective. By doing so, the supervisor renders rules and policies sensible guidelines for action and not arbitrary company decrees.

INCONSISTENT APPLICATION OF DISCIPLINE

A supervisor can gain the respect, support, and willing assistance of subordinates in enforcing rules and policies if the supervisor explains the rules properly. The rules and policies must apply to all and be fairly enforced without bias or favoritism, which can lead to other issues within the organization. For example: penalizing one employee for an offense that others have committed without punishment or reprimand, or cracking down one week and letting "anything go" the next week – both are sure ways to destroy discipline and morale in the organization. Employees expect stability in leadership. Lack of uniformity in the administration of discipline causes dissatisfaction and unrest.

Endnotes

Alfred Adler, *What Life Should Mean to You*, (London: Allen & Unwin, 1932): p. 55.

Chapter 4

Applying Human Relation Principles as a Supervisor

"Training and development must be built into the enterprise on all levels--training and development that never stop"

-Peter F. Drucker

A supervisor may know the technical aspects of their job thoroughly, but unless they like people, know what people respond to, and accept people as they are, then all of the supervisor's knowledge as a technician will be of little avail. The supervisor's actions and conduct must inspire confidence, responsibility, and mutual understanding from employees.

The age-old test of supervisory efficiency is the ability to place oneself in another person's position and, thereby, arrive at a proper understanding. Technicians are builders of things, but a supervisor must also be a builder of people, and their ability is measured in those terms alone. Of first importance is the supervisor's understanding of what the subordinates (workers) will respond to. Human nature has not changed much in the last 2000 years, as men and women respond to certain stimuli to align their internal or external wants, needs, and desires. For example, some of the basic elements for motivation spring from:

Ambition	Fair play
Confidence	Personal interest
Consideration	Pride
Consistency	Responsibility
Courtesy	Self-respect
Constructive criticism	Setting an example

Ambition - America has offered the greatest opportunity for the expression or development of ambition because, in America, each person is permitted to find their own level of success according to their own ability. The ambitious person is interested in three things:

1. Completing whatever task is assigned well;
2. Qualifying for a better job;
3. Developing an outside interest or hobby as a means of expression.

A supervisor must be aware of ambition employees, and can help make them successful in the following ways:

1. Finding the right person for the job;
2. Filling vacancies by promoting within the company;
3. Encouraging employees to improve themselves outside their work even though it is not directly related to their jobs;
4. Giving employees the proper training on the job so they can take pride in doing it well;
5. Training employees to do more than one job;
6. Remembering that, if you cannot find the employee a better job within your department, you should help the employee get a better job in another department;
7. Assisting new employees in acquiring the right types of training or vocational guidance;
8. Never standing in the way of anyone's advancement;
9. Never giving false hope for advancement;
10. Recognizing limitations for advancement and encouraging outside interests.

Confidence – Confidence is a contagious quality which every organizational leader must possess. If a supervisor does not have confidence, then they must assume it to inspire others. These points will help:

1. Keep promises, even if they are difficult;
2. Be a person of your word and never make promises which cannot be kept;
3. Show that you have confidence in your people;
4. Do not ask them to do anything you would not willingly to do yourself;
5. Be on the job when trouble develops;
6. Do not jump to conclusions about the conduct of your employees;
7. Give every person a fair deal;
8. Under no circumstances pull a "fast one" over on your employees.

Consideration – In showing consideration for your employees, an efficient supervisor will:

1. Treat everyone equally;
2. Be friendly and understanding of the employees' problems;
3. Know what's going on in the department at all times;
4. If work is to be done outside of regular hours, learn how it will affect each employee's personal plans;

5. Do not expect the impossible;
6. Be empathetic when sickness or misfortune occurs in an employee's personal life.

Consistency – Consistency is essential to high morale. In order to develop consistency, a supervisor should:

1. Be approachable;
2. Be consistent in telling one person the same thing, not giving different answers to the same question with different people;
3. Have standards of discipline and performance, and stick to them;
4. Keep cool in an argument or disagreement;
5. Keep their voice down;
6. Be able to overlook little things that do not merit any intervention;
7. Watch their health and don't become overtired or irritable;
8. Not jump to conclusions but instead get all the facts.

Courtesy – Everyone will find that politeness pays dividends; this is especially true for a supervisor:

1. Supervisors should have a friendly "good morning" and "good night" for each of their employees;
2. Supervisors should not permit employees to know when they feel a sense of low moral or

other negative emotions, either personal or professional;

3. Supervisors should avoid sarcasm or ridicule;
4. Supervisors should not talk negatively about others in lesser or higher positions.

Constructive criticism – Few people like criticism, regardless of its nature. One of the difficult tasks of a supervisor is to criticize and still retain the goodwill of the criticized. It is necessary at times for each of us to receive criticism.

1. Choose the right time to talk with the employee. Be sure they do not have something else on their mind;
2. Decide what you wish to say in advance. Have examples to illustrate your points;
3. Intersperse your criticism with praise of their good qualities in order to lead them to a receptive frame of mind;
4. Don't criticize all the employee's bad points at once. Discuss one or two shortcomings at a time;
5. Never permit the employee to leave discouraged. Make it clear that your interest in them is your only purpose in discussing the matter;
6. Don't speak in generalities. Get to the point;
7. Follow-up immediately with a friendly attitude to show that you hold no grudges;
8. Remember: criticize the work, not the person.

Fair play – In the workplace, more attention will be given to the elements of fair play than others. For example, an employee with special needs might require certain accommodation within the workplace. Others might misconstrue this element as unfair. The supervisor must clearly communicate to employees the differences within the workplace on a case-by-case basis. The supervisor should treat each employee uniformly based on similar skills, abilities, and circumstances. Although some elements are not under the direct control of the supervisor, they should understand what fair play includes:

1. Raises, wages, and promotions should be regular and uniform.
2. Work assignments should be done on the basis of ability alone.
3. Discipline should be administered uniformly to everyone.
4. Overtime should be evenly distributed (perhaps according to agreement).
5. Transfers and promotions should not be made on the basis of friendship.
6. Time off should be given to everyone alike, and not to favorites.

Personal interest – A supervisor has a better opportunity to know his or his people through their personal interests than in any other way. If you do not have a genuine interest in people that you supervisor than it will be difficult to lead. A company bowling activity or other function can help connect with people and share common interests.

Pride – People take pride in different things. Some have pride in their ancestry or lineage. Some take pride in appearance and others in achievement. In order to develop pride in employees, it is necessary to first understand them. Some elements to consider are as follows:

1. See that proper tools and the equipment necessary to the job are available.
2. Give your employees proper instruction.
3. Put your own job knowledge at their disposal.
4. Give employees a chance to learn more than one job.
5. Commend employees for a job well done.
6. Put important problems up to employees for suggestions. Ask their opinion.
7. Use established employees to instruct new hires.
8. Develop job interest by:
   a. Displaying a person's name over their office door, desk area, or workstation.
   b. Using a bulletin board or electronic suggestion boxes.
   c. Posting comparative standings or company dashboards on performance metrics (costs, output, defects, sales, etc.).

d. Do not use commands or orders when it is possible to use suggestions or directions.

Responsibility – Although some supervisors fear responsibility, it is only through its acceptance that growth occurs. Here are some factors:

1. Use the bulletin board or company dashboard to tell your employees about term performance metrics (waste, defects, spoilage, cost of repairs, delivery dates, critical deadlines, production schedules, etc.).
2. Hold departmental meetings to talk things over.
3. Make every person feel they are their own instructor.
4. Show your employees the importance of their work and the big picture about the organization and its operation.
5. Arrange to have employees tour the entire organization, factory, plant, or other areas to observe all operations.
6. Share your responsibility with them.

Self-Respect – These things will bring self-respect:

1. Provide and maintain good working conditions and personal conveniences.
2. Insist upon high standards of departmental orderliness and cleanliness.

3. Encourage suggestions.
4. See that each person understands the purpose of their job and how it contributes to the overall picture of the organization.
5. Help each person gain some personal satisfaction from their job.
6. Talk things over with your employees. Make them feel like part of a team.

Setting an Example – A supervisor sets the example for employees by his or her behaviors. For instance:

1. Do not ask anyone to do anything you would not do yourself.
2. Discard such phrases as "that is good enough," "I guess," or " I hope that will get by." Use phrases that will inspire others to think for themselves and be proactive in the best interest of the company.
3. Insist upon definite standards of performance, quality, quantity, and general housekeeping administrative items.
4. Be firm, but fair.
5. Work overtime if you asked your employees to.
6. Keep a friendly, cheerful attitude toward your problems and life in general.
7. Avoid destructive criticism and the peddling of gossip about the organization or personnel.
8. Stop rumors by investigation.

A supervisor is not a faultfinder. Supervisors constantly look for the good in their department, organization, and the people with whom they associate. Remember: if you don't practice it, you don't believe it.

Endnotes

Peter F. Drucker, *The Essential Drucker: The Best of Sixty Years of Peter Drucker's Essential Writings on Management*, (New York: Harper Business, Reissue, 2008): p.11.

Chapter 5

THE PROPER BEGINNING

"Smile…Give honest, sincere appreciation…Arouse in the other person an eager want…Become genuinely interested in other people…Remember that a person's name is to that person the most important sound in any language"

-DALE CARNEGIE (1936)*

In order to thoroughly understand problems that affect workers, it is imperative to begin instruction the first day on the job. Some supervisors have the wrong attitude toward new workers. Many supervisors assume that a new worker approaches the job with an arrogance that, if permitted, will spoil the employee's usefulness and that, if not properly subdued at the outset, the employee will not become an efficient worker.

It has been found that absenteeism, labor turnover, and general efficiency have already been determined to a great extent by a worker's first day on the job. First impressions are lasting. You no doubt can recall the first day you began work. There have been many other days since then which you do not recall, but the people you met and the things which occurred to you when you began your first day's work you remember in detail. The reason for this is simple. People are not at ease when they are in new surroundings and among people with whom they are not acquainted. A kind word, a little encouragement, a bit of understanding will go further on the first day of work than it will at any other time.

A supervisor is in a very enviable position when meeting the new employee on the first day on the job. It is possible to gain more goodwill on that particular day than at any other time. The following points should be remembered in getting a worker off to the right start:

1. Greet employees cordially.
2. Show a sincere and genuine interest in employees.
3. Ask questions about things in which the employee is interested.

4. Sell the employee on the importance of the job they will do.

5. Sell the employee on the company with which they are associated.

6. Introduce the employee to the other employees with whom they will work.

7. Show the employee around the department.

8. Tell the employee why their job is important in the overall picture of the department and company.

9. Do not talk down to new employees. Let them know they are important.

If these points are followed in a serious, sincere manner, you will have successfully started the new employee on their way to becoming an efficient worker. Even though you may think you are busy, it is difficult to imagine anything more important than getting your new employee off to the right start. In this new employee, you have a pillar for your supervisory foundation. Make it a good one.

Endnotes

1. Dale Carnegie, *How To Win Friend and Influence People*, (New York: Simon & Schuster, Inc., 1936).

* Dale Carnegie pointed out in his classic volume, *How To Win Friends and Influence People*, (New York: Simon & Schuster, Inc., 1936), an understanding of human nature through the underlying principles of dealing with people so that they feel important and appreciated.

Chapter 6

Instructing The Worker

"Every manager must motivate and encourage employees, somehow reconciling their individual needs with the goals of the organization"

-Henry Mintzberg

A large portion of the supervisor's time is consumed by instructing others. Over time, the supervisor becomes a better instructor as they improve their supervisory abilities. It is presumed by some authorities that a supervisor's efficiency is in direct proportion to their ability to instruct others. Many methods of instruction have been used in the past, but the method most generally employed with the greatest degree of success has been a combination of telling, showing, and doing. In other words, before a learner begins to learn a new job, they should be put in a receptive mood. The learner's attitude and receptiveness to learning the job's responsibilities influence the speed at which they will develop.

The next step after preparing the learner is to show them how to do the job. In this, the supervisor actually performs the task, while simultaneously explaining in detail the steps and key points involved. To ensure the employee's attentiveness, it is well-advised to ask to determine how the instruction is received. The next step is to have the employee perform the task and explain it as they do so. After that, the supervisor should allow the employee to work individually, first explaining the importance of the job, particularly safety, and other factors which directly affect the employee. The learner should be constantly reminded of the importance of the job they do and how it reflects their credibility. Care should be taken on the part of the supervisor not to make promises which cannot be fulfilled.

If the job is technical and long, it should be broken down into parts, with the easy parts given first. This is the first step in developing confidence in the learner. As confidence is developed, the learner becomes sure of themselves and their mind is free, then, to grasp the more difficult parts which follow. In asking questions regarding the worker's understanding of the job, it is important to ask questions which cannot be answered with a "yes" or "no." Use the "why," "what," "when," "where," "how," and "who" types of questions that require more explanation. In this way, the supervisor will be able to determine any pitfalls that might confuse the learner.

There are several things to do in training any new employee, which are of prime importance. These are:

1. Under no circumstances should the supervisor allow a new employee to fail on their first job.
2. Teach the employee the easy parts of the job first to develop confidence.
3. Select the right person to instruct the learner.
4. Put the learner in the right frame of mind before beginning instruction.
5. Sell the employee on the importance of the job they do.
6. Follow-up closely the first day and the first week to see that the learner is in a happy frame of mind.
7. Make the new employee feel that they belong. Tell them why their job is important, and how it fits into the overall department and company picture.
8. In instruction, use as many of the senses as possible. Employ *seeing* and *hearing* primarily.
9. Don't treat all learners alike. Recognize their individuality.

10. Teach them only that which they do not already know, but check to make sure you are correct in your assumptions.
11. Stress a healthy and safe work environment at all times.

Endnotes

Henry Mintzberg, *The Manager's Job: Folklore and Fact* (New York: Harvard Business Publishing (HBP), Harvard Business Review, March-April, 1990): 168.

The Supervisor's Guide to

HUMAN RELATIONS AND COMMUNICATION

Chapter 7

GRIEVANCES

*"It is bad enough to have a real grievance
of any kind—it is worse when one
must bear it on an empty stomach"*

-HORATIO ALGER, JR. *(1911)*

A grievance is defined as "anything a person thinks is wrong or unfair." Grievances can be purely imaginary. A large percentage of grievances are invalid. Whenever you have people working together, you are bound to have competitions, dissatisfactions, arguments, and in fact, oppositions to the common cause. These mental disturbances might be called irritations or grievances. Oftentimes, when slight irritations are nipped in the bud (resolved before beginning), the grievances that otherwise would have resulted are avoided.

When one is worried about home conditions or relatives, it is difficult to assume an attitude of sunshine and rosiness on the job. As supervisors, we often cannot stop these worries, but we can understand them and, thereby, deal with the worker in a more sensible manner. It will help supervisors to understand why people sometimes act as they do.

Grievances usually result from minor complaints and irritations that have been ignored or left unresolved by the supervisor. These irritations or grievances grow larger as they age. They gain size and momentum like a snowball rolling down a hill; ultimately, they could result in a loss of hundreds of work hours or even a factory shutdown. Grievances will result in the following:

1. Slow work productivity;
2. Consume time;
3. Raise departmental costs;
4. Increase absenteeism;
5. Increase labor turnover;
6. Increase training and development costs;
7. Lower morale;
8. Erode trust;
9. Increase accidents;
10. Cause poor housekeeping.

The following are reasons a supervisor should handle irritations and grievances when they arise:

1. The supervisor is closer to the worker than anyone else.
2. The supervisor can "nip" the irritation in the "bud."
3. Intervention increases the supervisor's prestige with management.
4. Intervention helps the supervisor develop self-confidence.
5. Intervention builds morale among workers.
6. Intervention maintains quantity and quality of work.
7. Intervention lowers costs.
8. Intervention retains workers.

Grievances should be handled promptly because it is disturbing to workers' attitudes and will grow in importance the longer delayed. Prompt handling improves workers' attitudes toward the supervisor. The following are suggested methods for handling grievances:

1. Put the worker at ease. Make them feel they have a right to come to you.
2. Hear their full story – irritations sometimes disappear in the telling.
3. Don't interrupt.

4. Don't raise your voice; be calm, patient, and tolerant.
5. Encourage the worker retell their story for clarification.
6. Question the worker on major points.
7. Try to locate the root of the problem since complaints may be only symptoms of some other concern.
8. Review the record.
9. Talk with other individuals involved.
10. Get the opinions and feelings of others.
11. Be sure to get the whole story.
12. Fit the facts together.
13. Consider the facts' bearing on each other.
14. What possible actions are there? What are the alternatives?
15. Take action. Make a decision promply.
16. Inform the worker promptly. Don't take for granted that they know your decision.
17. Help the employee save face, if humanly possible.
18. Build the worker up, but don't use flattery; be genuine and sincere.
19. If possible, yield on a trivial point.
20. Accept the consequences of your decisions.

This approach can be used effectively to handle an irritation, complaint, or major grievance (if you have been given the authority to handle a major grievance). The pattern is the same in each case, and how thoroughly you go into the details outlined in each step will depend upon the importance and size of the problem.

It should always be remembered that no grievance, regardless of size or importance, is ever settled until the worker has been informed of the decision which has been made – and sold on the fairness of it, if the decision is adverse.

Each individual and every supervisor who had any-thing to do with making the decision is responsible. The supervisor who handled the grievance originally should be notified, and whenever possible, the original supervisor should be the one who notifies the worker.

Whatever method used, a process must be followed to inform the worker. If the worker isn't informed, they will have another grievance in addition to the original one. Following a process of notification will keep your supervisory issues from festering.

Endnotes

Horatio Alger, Jr., *From Farm to Fortune,* (New York: The New York Book Company, 1911).

Chapter 8

Habits, Listening, and Speaking

*"You can make more friends in two
months by becoming more interested in
other people than you can in two years
by trying to get people interested in you"*

-DALE CARNEGIE*

A habit is said to be an automatic action set into motion without conscious effort. Shifting the gears of a car is a fair example; others include tying shoelaces or many of the daily activities in which we engage.

When we have reached middle life, we are usually victims of habits developed over long periods of time. These habits may either be physical or mental. It has been proven that men 40 to 50 years of age, or even into 60 years of age, can learn just as quickly as those 18- to 20 years old. The older person must unlearn a great deal before beginning to learn something new. These habits form a mental model for the way of looking at the world. When old habits impede learning, the progress of the younger or older person are limited from reaching its full potential.

Any person can learn if they first recognize the need and create a desire to learn. Habits which aid us in the performance of our work are obviously useful. For example, when you learned to shift gears in a car, you did exactly the same things that you do now, yet the difference in the time required is considerable. The reduction in time did not come about by learning a new method, but by the elimination of false starts.

A *false start* is any point in an operation where a decision must be made. After the decisions have been made over and over again, the same way, they are no longer required, and then the time consumed by those decisions is eliminated, which accounts for the decrease in time required. When false starts are eliminated, the operation can be called a habit; things done correctly through habit are done faster and, usually, better.

Through repetition or constant use, the brain cells that control an operation are believed to grow larger from repeated exertion. These things are helpful in learning or in habit formation:

1. Nothing can be learned without practice.
2. All learning requires practice.
3. Practice is doing; doing is practice.
4. The inevitable result of practice is learning.
5. Anything we practice will be learned.
6. Practice is essential to learning.
7. Skill requires much practice.
8. There is a limit to all accomplishment, and we may reach a point beyond which we cannot go, regardless of practice.
9. Our capacity to learn will determine our degree of proficiency.
10. All individuals vary in their capacities for learning.
11. General intelligence is the determining factor in the potential degree of proficiency.
12. High general intelligence is required for rapid learning.
13. Intentions do not count in learning. Only what we do is learned, regardless of intentions.
14. Motivation, self-confidence, and willingness to learn are great attributes, but capacities for learning vary from person to person.

It is important to analyze our learning and determine whether we are learning what we desired or whether we are practicing something else. We should bring our *doing* in line with our *intentions* in order to learn that which we desire. In order to retain learning, we must practice it regularly. It is desirable to over-learn in order to remember.

In order to break a habit, all we need do is to forget; that is, do not practice the habit. This is not so easily accomplished, however, and it is advisable, oftentimes, to substitute a new habit for the one being discarded. According to William James[1], noted psychologist, the following rules should be followed to break a habit:

1. Take care to launch yourself with as strong and definite an initiative as possible on the new habit.
2. Never allow an exception to occur until the new habit is securely rooted in your life.
3. Seize the first possible opportunity to shift your actions in the direction of the habit you aspire to gain, in every resolution you make and every emotional prompting you experience.
4. Keep your faculties for effort alive with a little gratuitous exercise each day.

In order to form a habit or break one, it is necessary to have the right attitude towards it. Attitudes are influenced by a person's physical condition, mental condition, or environment. The attitudes of employees are determined by many influencing factors:

1. Job security;
2. The way they are treated by management;

3.   Their rate of pay;
4.   How they perceive their jobs;
5.   Their home environments.

Of all these factors, you, their supervisor, have major control of only one factor – that is, the way the employees feel about his or her employer. If the employee's experiences with you reveal your indecision, then the employee may feel all management is indecisive. If a member of your department or unit sees you as cold and aloof, then they may conclude that all management is cold and aloof. Consequently, your actions and attitudes as perceived by employees tell them what to think about you and the company in general.

One may wonder and reflect upon why working men or women who have been on the job for a number of years look to you, their supervisor, for determination of their attitudes towards management and the company. For that newly-minted supervisor with no years of experience, it can be an equally daunting task to reflect the attitudes of management and the company. By default, the supervisor's position is one of authority and responsibility; hence, the owner of authority holds the determination of employees' attitudes since you, as the supervisor, are established as a pacesetter or standard-bearer for the organization. Recognize that you hold a position of responsibility wherein your actions, behavior, demeanor, enthusiasm, and dedication will be constantly observed by employees as they attempt to determine their attitudes about you and management generally.

Success and security must be a matter of mutual interest to both the company and the employees. Management cannot be successful without the human resource capital found in every employee, and employees cannot obtain a measure of security without successful management.

BEING AWARE

Being cognizant of *what's going on* in the minds and actions of employees enables the supervisor to better understand what the "real" problems are. If there is an area in need of settlement, or if there is merit in the complaint of an employee, the supervisor should not approach the problem with the attitude of *How do I defend myself or my company?* Rather, the supervisor's approach should involve the question of *How do I settle this?* The settlement should be consistent with the agreement and/or local practices or procedures. Experience has proven that most human relations problems in the workplace are best solved between the supervisor and employee. At this level, each party is closer to the problem and is in a position to more fully understand the other's viewpoint than is the case with subsequent steps of any grievance procedure. If an employee is entitled to something based on the agreement, make an effort to supply it. Be fair. Regard anything that is the employee's as the employee's.

Supervisors must understand that the way their employees feel about them will greatly influence the way they feel about the company in general.

LISTENING

When we start talking, we often cease to listen in that large sense of being attuned to the other person's unspoken reactions and attitudes. Even more serious is the fact that we are all guilty, at times, of inattentiveness when others attempt to communicate with us. Listening is one of the most important, most difficult, and most neglected skills in communication. It demands that we concentrate not only on the explicit meanings another person expresses, but also on the implicit meanings, unspoken words, and undertones that may be far more significant. Thus, we must learn to listen with the inner ear if we are to know the inner person.

Perhaps we think listening is a simple matter. The fact that so few people listen proves it is not so simple. It is estimated that well over 50% of daily orders in business given by superiors are misunderstood. There is more to listening than keeping one's own mouth closed while the other speaks. The skill of listening cannot be acquired in six easy lessons. We might, however, consider the obstacles to effective listening and then take positive steps to eliminate these obstacles.

The first and most important obstacle is *unawareness of the importance of listening*. Becoming thoroughly convinced of the importance of listening is half the battle. *Fatigue* and *illness* are obstacles to listening. *Tension* is another obstacle. People are unpredictable. When we don't know how to deal with them, we become tense. An appearance of tension may close the lines of communication. We must appear relaxed when a person talks with us in our offices or work area. Drumming on the desk, continuously adjusting glasses, stroking the chin, or adjusting clothing -- such mannerisms will discourage people from expressing themselves. Instead, the employee will become more concerned with watching than with talking, and will sense immediately your lack of attentiveness. *Impatience* is an obstacle. We cannot hurry a person speaking to us. We must let them say what they have to say at their own pace.

Preoccupation is an obstacle which blocks communication. If we have our next mortgage payment in mind while someone speaks to us, it is impossible to understand. We must have empathy with the other person. Empathy is simply allowing oneself to see the other person's viewpoint or, as the saying goes, "put yourself in the other person's shoes." *Egocentricity* is another barrier. Egocentric people think only of themselves. They cannot listen. We must exalt the "you" and dethrone the "I" if we are to listen effectively.

Another obstacle is *prejudice*. *Prejudice* has no place in the life of a supervisor. Prejudice against a person deadens us. Prejudice prevents us from dealing fairly with people. We must not prejudge a person before we hear what they have to say.

Lastly, *distraction* is an obstacle. Too many objects in view during conversation distract both worker and supervisor. A stack of important papers on the middle of the desk is a great temptation, letting the mind wander back to those important matters. Pictures also distract attention, and doodling is almost a personal affront to the visitor. If we clear the desk, chances are good that both will be able to concentrate on the matter at hand. We should remember to look the person who speaks to us in the eyes. *A personal reflection as found in the Bible passage Matthew 6:22.* We know how disconcerting it feels to find a superior looking in another direction when we enter their office at their request. It is even more disconcerting when the superior continues to look in another direction while we talk.

Attempting to do *two things at once* has a deadly effect on communication. We cannot talk and listen at the same time, or read and listen at the same time, or listen to two different things simultaneously. Effective listening requires undivided attention.

It is well to remember that "a word" can have several different meanings. If we are to avoid misunderstandings, we must do more than superficially hear the speaker's words. We must try to understand the full and exact meaning of all the words taken together. Complete attention is vital.

Some of us *plan our answers while the other person is speaking*. Again, we cannot do two things at once. We cannot listen and plan a reply at the same time. We should wait until we have heard the other person finish before deciding on a rejoinder. We cannot be buck-passers, meaning we cannot blame the other person for breakdowns in communication. It is easy to exonerate ourselves, but then our communication will not improve. *Communication is management's responsibility*. We must work at it.

It would do well to mention just one last barrier to effective listening that will seldom fool anyone: *pretending to listen*. No matter how good we may think we are at acting, people can see through it. **A personal reflection as found in the Bible passage Matthew 5:8.** Sooner or later in the conversation, we will be forced to ask the classic question, "What did you say?" and then we will learn that listening requires sincerity.

We have not thought about listening as a tool. We cannot see, hear, or touch the listening tool. Perhaps its intangibility explains our neglect. Listening is a difficult tool to use, but neither past neglect nor present difficulties should deter us from learning to use one of management's most important tools.

SPEAKING

A supervisor's prime responsibility is to get things done through other people. However sound your ideas or well-reasoned your decisions, they become effective only when they are transmitted to others and achieve the desired action or reaction. Communication, therefore, is your most vital supervisory tool.

On the job, we communicate not only with words but through attitudes and actions because communication encompasses all human behavior that results in an exchange of meaning. How well you manage depends on how well you communicate in this broad sense.

The following suggestions are designed to help improve supervisory skills by improving communication skills — with supervisors, subordinates, and associates.

1. *Clarify your ideas before communicating.*
   a. The more systematically we analyze the problem or idea being communicated, the clearer it becomes. This is the first step toward effective communication. Many communications fail because of inadequate planning. Good planning considers the goals and attitudes of those who you will communicate with and those who are affected by it.
2. *Examine the true purpose of each communication.*
   a. Before you communicate, ask yourself what you really want to accomplish with your message. Do you want to obtain information?

Initiate action? Change another person's attitude? Identify your most important goal and then adapt your language, tone, and total approach to serve that specific objective. Don't try to accomplish too much with each communication. The sharper the focus of your message, the greater its chances of success.

3. *Consider the physical setting whenever you communicate.*

   a. Meaning and intent are conveyed by more than words alone. Many other factors influence the overall impact of a communication, and the supervisor must be sensitive to the total setting in which communication occurs. For example, consider your sense of *timing*, i.e., the circumstances under which you make an announcement or render a decision. The *physical setting*, meaning whether you communicate in private and the *social climate* that pervades work relationships within the company or a department set the tone of its communications; *custom and past practice* involve the degree to which your communication conforms to, or departs from, the expectations of your audience. Be constantly aware of the total setting in which you communicate. The supervisor must be capable of adapting to its environment to communicate successful.

4. *Consult with others, where appropriate, in planning communication.*
    a. Frequently, it is desirable or necessary to seek the participation of others in planning a communication or developing the facts on which it's based. Such consultation often helps by lending additional insight and objectivity to your message. Moreover, those who have helped you plan your communication will give it their active support.

5. *While you communicate, be mindful of the overtones as well as the basic content of your message.*
    a. Your tone of voice, expression, apparent receptiveness to the responses of others all have tremendous impact on those you wish to reach. Frequently overlooked, these subtleties of communication often affect a listener's reaction to a message even more than its basic content. Similarly, your choice of language, particularly your awareness of the fine shades of meaning and emotion in the words you use, pre-determines in large part the reactions of your listeners.

6. *Take the opportunity, when it arises, to convey something of help or value to the receiver.*
    a. Consideration of the other person's interests and needs, the habit of trying to look at things from the other person's viewpoint, will

frequently highlight opportunities to convey something of immediate benefit or long-term value to the person. People on the job are most responsive to the supervisor whose messages take their own interests into account.

7. *Follow-up on your communication.*

    a. Our best efforts at communication may be wasted, and we may never know whether we have succeeded in expressing our true meaning and intent, if we do not follow-up to see how well we have expressed our message to others. This you can do by asking questions, encouraging the receiver to express their reactions, following-up with contacts, and subsequent review of performance. Make certain that every important communication has "feedback" so that complete understanding and appropriate action result.

8. *Communicate for tomorrow as well as today.*

    a. While communication is aimed at meeting the demands of an immediate situation along with expectations established from past interactions, it is important to keep in mind how this communication will affect events in the future as well. Thus, maintain consistency in those receiving the communications; but, most important, they must also be consistent with long-term interests and goals of the company.

For example, it is not easy to communicate frankly on such matters as poor performance or the shortcomings of a loyal subordinate, but postponing disagreeable communication makes communicating more difficult in the long run and is actually unfair to subordinates and the company.

9. *Be sure your actions support your communication.*
   a. In the final analysis, the most persuasive kind of communication is not what is said but what is done. When a supervisor's actions or attitude contradicts their words, one tends to discount or avoid what they say. This means that good supervisory practice – such as clear assignment of responsibility and authority, fair rewards for effort, and sound policy accountability – serves to communicate more than all the gifts of oration.

10. *Last, but by no means least, always be more willing to listen than to speak.* Seek not only to be understood, but to understand others and keep control of your emotions.

Endnotes

1. William James, *The Principles of Psychology*, (New York: Henry Holt & Company, 1890): 1 (1).
2. Dale Carnegie, *How To Win Friend and Influence People*, (New York: Simon & Schuster, Inc., 1936)
3. Matthew 6:22 (written perhaps from AD 40 – AD 100). All translations.
4. Matthew 5:8 (written perhaps from AD 40 – AD 100). All translations.
5. James 1:19 (written perhaps from AD 40 – AD 100). All translations.

Chapter 9

THE PERFORMANCE APPRAISAL

*"The achievements of an organization
are the results of the combined
effort of each individual."*

-*VINCE LOMBARDI*

Many companies use the terms *performance appraisal*, *performance management*, *90-day probation period*, and *annual employee review* to capture the work activities of employees. A company's success can be defined by measurable outcomes specific to the company's goals, the role of managers, performance indicators at the different departmental levels, and internal processes (correctly or incorrectly) used to ensure its success. Examples of these processes include the way people design, build, assemble, service, and maintain products and services for the company. As a supervisor, you are on the frontlines of ensuring that your subordinates are performing their work tasks and meeting the objectives of the company. The most effective performance appraisal review processes occur year-round, not just during the end-of-year requirement for employees. A supervisor who is cognitive of their people will check-in periodically throughout the year and make the necessary corrections for the employee and company to succeed. A supervisor could suggest a training class or offer a one-on-one quarterly review so the employee has a clear picture of the needs of the company. A supervisor at a smaller company might find an informal weekly- or month-in-review helpful for employees. Employees feel connected with the company when they feel their contributions matter to the company.

An effective organization is the lifeblood to many companies, no matter the size. The value created by employees through work manifests itself throughout the business, and supervisors lead the management with an environment that defines the heart and soul of the organization.

In order for employees to accept the notion of *this is the way things get done around here*, they must equally believe in the managers who set the tone. This has much to do with culture and an acceptable environment that lives and breathes as the pulse of a company people *want* to work for. A supervisor is the tone-setter for this life. Similarly, employees find the performance appraisal process useless unless the supervisor takes on the importance of the review process. It must be more than checking a few boxes in the paperwork. Historically, performance appraisal reviews have failed to add much value to companies. Many employees believe the flaw in the performance appraisal review process lies with the supervisors, while the supervisors believe the flaws lie with the human resources department, the upper-level managers, or owners.

A supervisor can change the company culture and value associated with performance appraisal reviews of employees.

Effective supervisors are those who can:

1. *Establish an environment in which people can advance* – Build an environment in which the company's actions reflect value created by:
    * demonstrating the company's values in behaviors, actions, and relationships that align with decisions;
    * creating a sense of shared ownership and accountability among employees;
    * encouraging employee to perform at their full potential by providing development,

coaching, and rewards and consequences for all levels of performance;

* inspiring and aligning human resources by communicating a compelling vision;

* encouraging employees to embrace change and quickly adapt to new ways of doing business.

2. *Create knowledgeable workers who exemplify the knowledge required to lead or contribute to the viability of the company.*

Effective, knowledgeable workers are those who have:

* product or service knowledge.
* business and finance knowledge.
* market/industry knowledge.
* multinational knowledge.

The knowledgeable worker can:

* evaluate and integrate information to create critical action items;

* engage in decision-making based on an understanding of the core competencies of the company;

* determine and balance short-term and long-term goals that align with all stakeholders;

* identify opportunities and threats;

* encourage new ideas and reward risk versus reward relevant to performance and development objectives;

     ★ be action-oriented and support decision-making in a dynamic environment;

     ★ be accountable and take personal responsibility for decisions, regardless of outcome;

     ★ make timely decisions and take corrective action if things do not go as planned.

3. *Build and sustain partnerships by delivering customer value.*

Effective supervisors are those who can:

     ★ create, develop and maintain strategic alliances, partnerships, and relationships that result in cross-organizational cooperation;

     ★ cooperate internally to compete externally;

     ★ align one's work with that of related teams;

     ★ utilize all resources available across the organization.

THE SUPERVISOR'S ROLE IN THE PERFORMANCE APPRAISAL

The supervisor's role in the performance appraisal process is to share an equal part of the employee's review. Training and development needs must align with the employee's interests and development plan.

For example:

     ★ What specific skills, knowledge, behaviors, or capabilities need to be developed to enhance the individual's ability?

* How does the individual's ability align with performance objectives and/or job requirements?
* Can each development objective demonstrate specific outcomes relevant to each performance objective and/or job requirement?

As a supervisor, you are accountable for each subordinate. Many workers are asked *to know more* and *do more* than in past work environments. Supervisors have the responsibility to the subordinate to provide an environment that is safe, efficient, positive, and results-oriented. A supervisor can be proactive in developing an employee action plan to improve the performance of their employees.

For example the supervisor can help guide employees in 1.) identification of action plan, 2.) identification of resources needed, 3.) identification of roadblocks and anticipated barriers, and 4.) determination of how results will be measured toward the goals/objectives outlined upon by the supervisor.

Specific action steps may include:

* job assignments
* coaching
* training and education
* organizational/work redesign

Supervisor's must articulate and encourage the specific actions necessary to help subordinates achieve each of the objectives in employees' development plan. Such actions reflect the qualities of leadership and are part of the human relations function of the performance appraisal process.

Specific steps taken by a supervisor in employees' development plan are:

* develop or update job descriptions for employees;
* actively participate in training and demonstrate competency based on training received;
* know and implement compliance requirements in the work area;
* know and follow established, job-specific and facility-wide policies and procedures.

There should be a summary of the overall annual performance plan to show the extent to which the employee has achieved each performance measure and developed during the period of review. The fallacy that has challenged the overall annual performance appraisal process is when supervisors lack a *sincere and genuine* insight for relationship-building with subordinates. This undermines the entire process when employee trust is lost and they do not feel valued or believe in the performance appraisal process. Employees may question the review process openly or privately to others, perhaps saying, "What does it matter, the pay raises are subjective and political?," "My supervisor rushes through my review without a care in the world," "It's all about getting the paperwork done to satisfy human resource compliances," "The owner decides the fate of us all," "If we only had a strong union representing the workers," or "A private company can do whatever it wants for the most part."

Supervisors must take the lead in order to communicate openly with employees to improve and build upon the performance appraisal process. Supervisors and employees are faced with many challenges and problems when dealing with the annual review. When more solutions are offered to human resource managers, then more supervisors will be able to meet the challenges in performance appraisal reviews for their company. A supervisor must acknowledge their people with appreciation for good work so employees feel like part of the company. Supervisors can create an environment that is met with genuine sincerity by employees in the annual performance review process. Additional criteria for individuals' performance and development objectives should also reflect affirmative action and diversity objectives as evident throughout the year. Affirmative action means taking positive steps towards creating a work environment free from all forms of discrimination. Specifically for supervisors, it means providing all employees with opportunities to make the most of their talents and aspirations. Asking for employee comments can be a challenge for open, honest and sincere thoughts between supervisors and employees, but it is highly recommended if one wants to be the supervisor who is most admired, respected, and who others go above and beyond for. Is that too much to ask of a person who holds the future of their subordinate? Let your light so shine before men, that they may see your good works. *A personal reflection as found in the Bible passage Matthew 5:16.*

Endnotes

1. Vince Lombardi, Quote retrieved from http://www.vincelombardi.com (The official website of Vince Lombardi, Family of Vince Lombardi, 2017).
2. Robert C. Preziosi, *The 2007 Pfeiffer Annual: Human Resource Management, Insights and Perspectives–Challenges and Solutions in Performance Management by Michael D. Santonino III*, (Pfeiffer publishing, 2006): pp. 235-244.
3. Matthew 5:16 (written perhaps from AD 40 – AD 100). All translations.

INDEX

ABOUT THE AUTHORS

Michael D. Santonino III received both his Doctor and Master of Business Administration from H. Wayne Huizenga School of Business and Entrepreneurship at Nova Southeastern University. He also holds an Electrical Engineering degree from the New York Institute of Technology. He is a management practitioner with more than 15 years of corporate experience working for military defense contractors and high-tech commercial corporations.

Frank J. Villa Jr. is the former CEO of the Colorado and Wyoming Railroad in Pueblo Colorado. He has more than 30 years in executive management, corporate training, negotiations and arbitration. He ran a successful Railroad Technical Training Service (RTTS) after retirement in supervisory training. He has no college degrees.

The Supervisor's Guide to

HUMAN RELATIONS AND COMMUNICATION

HOW TO BE A SUPERVISOR WITH OR WITHOUT AN EDUCATION OR EXPERIENCE!

Have you been catapulted to a supervisory position, but you have no clue how to manage people? Are you a small company that cannot afford a training and development program for supervisors?

Maybe you are tired of faking it or isolating yourself from your subordinates.

Now, here's a simple, straightforward, and practical supervisor's guide built around a few key principles that have existed for thousands of years....you don't need to hold an MBA or read management theory to understand that human relations and communication are the solutions to being a great supervisor without the extra baggage.

Michael D. Santonino III and Frank J.Villa Jr. take you through the areas most important to the practicing supervisor, offering training and development tips, suggestions, and ideas designed to improve skills as a supervisor in any business. This human relations and communication guide prepares you to deal with supervisory issues including: the supervisor's role, instructing workers, discipline, grievances, performance appraisals, new employee orientation, absenteeism, labor turnover, job security, and the general efficiency of workers. You'll discover ways to better understand yourself and how to be a well-respected supervisor.

If you want to improve your supervisory skills and earn the respect of your subordinates, *The Supervisor's Guide to Human Relations and Communication* gives you the building blocks you need to improve, leading to a happier workplace and more productive work environment for all.

> *"Value-creating companies such as Google, Intel, and Southwest Airlines develop their people to their full potential. While your firm may not be an industry giant (yet), you can still learn how to master the HR function with the practical guidelines provided by Dr. Michael Santonino and Mr. Frank Villa. This action-packed supervisor's manual quickly explains how to lead and leverage the talent within your organization to maximize productivity. Read it before your competitors do!"*

Art Weinstein, Ph.D., Professor of Marketing, Nova Southeastern University and author of Superior Customer Value.

NOTES

NOTES

NOTES

Made in the USA
Columbia, SC
11 October 2017